More than Survival

Complete Communication with God

LaVonne Masters

Masters Publishers

Scripture quotations are from the NEW KING JAMES VERSION of the Bible. Copyright © 1979, 1980, 1982, Thomas Nelson Publishers, Inc.

ISBN 13:978-1491258941

ISBN 10:1491258942

To my five grandchildren:
Jonathan Westerfield,
Christie Westerfield Wyatt, Jamie Westerfield Shores,
Victoria Ellis, and Elizabeth Ellis.
I love you all and pray you always
communicate with God every day!

Contents

1

Communication with God

Victoria, Elizabeth and I followed the people in the tour groups and took off our shoes and carefully placed them alongside all the hundreds of other shoes outside the Wat Phra Keo—the royal temple of the Emerald Buddha, one of the most venerated sites in Bangkok, Thailand. My husband and I were taking care of our granddaughters for five weeks as our daughter JoAnn and her husband Reid finished their classes for their Master's degrees in international education. To entertain the girls, I decided to take a few tours with them. We toured palaces and many other popular tourist sites. This particular tour included the Emerald Buddha—a carved image made of solid green jade and gold.

Now as we gingerly continued barefooted into the temple, Victoria, 9, and Elizabeth, 7, held onto each of my hands. I had some reservations about taking my granddaughters into a place where the belief system totally differed from ours, but I thought it might be a teaching opportunity.

As we entered, there were about a hundred people crowded near the front bowing on their knees, and some even prostrating themselves as they brought their petitions to the Emerald Buddha. Many of them prayed aloud.

It struck me as futility for all these intelligent-appearing people from all over the world to try to communicate with an image who did not hear them, see them, or talk to them.

I said quietly to my granddaughters, "To think, this god can't see, hear or talk."

Victoria added, "And he can't even grant their requests."

I realized she assessed the situation correctly and quickly. I really had no need to fear the girls would think this was the Almighty God or a representative of His. Victoria saw immediately that there was no communication or interaction with this image.

People around the world possess this deep need to fellowship and commune with the living God. Faithfully they will pray and offer sacrifices to gods or images. Often, because of the false gods inability to communicate, there may be misconceptions about the ability of the true God to communicate. Many consider this impossible.

Fellowship and complete communication with the living God are possible. It involves just five key features:

Choosing God, taking time with Him.

Loving God, getting to know who He is.

Conversing with God, listening and talking to Him.

Asking of God, learning how to ask of Him.

Winning with God, taking action for Him.

It is not mystical to commune with God. It is not difficult or time-consuming.

This communication with God plan is practical and easy. Anyone can do it because God meets us where we are as we are. God shows no favoritism. We don't have to exhibit a certain I.Q., belong to the preferred crowd, or grow up in the "right" culture. We don't have to assume a "religious" tone of voice, speak with pious-sounding words, or attain a certain spiritual level. The Bible says, "Draw near to God and He will draw near to you."

"You" includes everyone—you and me. He desires closeness with all of us. He's waiting to come to us with love and understanding.

Yet, He doesn't force us into nearness with Him. We're not marionettes. We have a choice—to choose fellowship with Him.

The Bible tells us about the importance of fellowship with God. God created us for this purpose. We are all searching for this kind of relationship. When we're not in communication with God, we're not fulfilled.

William Morris expressed this thought well when he said: "Fellowship is Heaven, and lack of fellowship is Hell; fellowship is life, and lack of fellowship is death."

With fellowship, with intimacy, we thrive. Intimacy with God satisfies.

J. B. Phillips said, "God is the great reality."

Fellowship with God, then, can be the greatest reality experience of our lives.

This reality of communication with God gives us ability to "more than survive."

God's primary plan for spiritual development is for us to communicate with Him, and this is a learning process. Then, best of all, our relationship with God brings benefits—the supplying of our basic needs.

Abraham Maslow developed the hierarchy of human needs. He taught that those needs were necessary in the development of human potential. They are: survival, security, love, self-esteem, self-actualization.

Psalm 34:10 tells us these needs can be a certainty by communication with God, "But those who seek the Lord shall not lack any good thing."

Seeking God and supplied needs become synonymous. We can't have one without the other.

This book consists of the five aspects of communication with God. Each part has three chapters that include the obstacle, the how-to, and the benefit for each feature of communication with God.

> Obstacle: dealing with glitches
> How-to: concise and practical options
> Benefit: fulfillment of human needs

Using the ideas in this book will change your life.

Part One: Choosing God

"Early will I seek you." Psalm 63:1

2

Obstacle: Sorting through the Maze

There is a book about a boy named Collin. In this story, Collin starts traveling in a maze. By trial and error and meeting many stone walls, he finally stumbles onto the center of the tangle. To his surprise he finds many people living there.

Immediately they inform Collin, "There is no way out of here."

This revelation stuns him, but he refuses to believe it, and determines to find a way. An idea strikes him, "Why not climb the wall and see if there is a way out."

After much persuasion, the people agree to help him by forming a human ladder against the wall. Then Collin carefully climbs to the top.

"You can see the whole network from here," Collin says. "We can walk on top of the wall. There is a way out. We can jump down right here," he shouts as he points below his feet.

As much as Collin tries, he can't convince any of the other people to come with him. They prefer to stay trapped by the maze rather than take the way out. So Collin gets out of the maze by jumping off the wall and continues on his journey alone.

We may feel trapped like the people in this story by a maze of things to do and wonder: Is there a way out?

Sort through your labyrinth by using three things that work for me: choosing priorities, evaluating activities, and eliminating activities.

Priorities

In a class of seventy-five single and married young adults that my husband and I were team-teaching we asked, "What do you consider the number one quest of your life?"

Most of the answers were: success, fulfillment, happiness, and financial freedom. One couple eagerly anticipated getting their kids raised so they could travel the country in a motor home. Less than ten percent named the pursuit of God as their priority.

One of our biggest obstacles is sifting through all our endeavors to the most important, because our lives demand we fill so many roles: parent, spouse, business expert, teacher, companion, chauffeur, gardener, and Christian. How do we know what to put first?

This is how I choose my priorities. I put communication with God as number one. This is not always easy. Some days and weeks I struggle with it, but I continue to pursue it as my priority.

My second priority is to my spouse, Ron. A marriage takes time, intimacy, and companionship. To make this possible, I choose to consider Ron more important to me than any other person or my ambitions.

My third priority is for my children, their spouses, and grandchildren. Children are treasures Ron and I will bring to God in eternity. The love, care, time, teaching, and our example make the difference in their lives. They are the fruits of our lives.

This is my priority list:

1. Communication with God
2. Spouse, Ron
3. Children and family

Using this list as a guide, alter it to fit you and your lifestyle. If you are single you have more flexibility with your list.

Evaluating activities

We are so busy, so involved in frantic activity. Our lives become a huge web that resembles a bureaucracy. Most agencies start out with a specific purpose and goal but when they add more departments and subtract none, they eventually cease to operate properly. The original function, then, becomes lost in robotics.

Our life doesn't have to be mired in details. We don't have to choose frenzied activity. We can choose to go back to simpler, happier lives with fewer activities.

Try slowing the pace with this method: Every six months or so list all your activities and responsibilities on a sheet of paper.

Ask yourself two questions:

1. Which of these activities will meet the spiritual needs of me and/or my family? Mark them with a check.
2. Which of these activities will meet the mental and physical needs of me and/or my family? Mark them with a check.

Eliminating activities

Now look at the list again and decide to lighten the load.

First, of those items checked, cross off some of the frivolous activities. Unimportant things have a way of sneaking in and crowding out the essential. Vance Havner called it "glorified piddling." It is preoccupation with the trivial.

For example, I eliminated watching too much television, unnecessary shopping trips, and limiting my reading time. I can spend hours doing nothing.

Second, of those items checked, cross off jobs others can do.

If you're swamped in your business, train and delegate some of your work to trusted employees. If you are a parent, you can organize your household. You can train your children to do household chores. When they become teenagers they can cook, clean their rooms, take care of their clothes, mow the yard, wash the car, and more. Every family member can learn to contribute.

Be careful of taking on too many volunteer jobs in the church and the community. If this has happened to you, look for replacements for some of these positions. Others may be just waiting to get involved.

We can't hold on to too many endeavors at once. It takes too much energy. We can end up grasping on to just residue of our lives.

Summing up, this is the process for sorting through priorities:

1. List priorities.
2. List all other activities and evaluate them.
3. Eliminate some things altogether.

Keep this list of priorities and activities for reference to remind yourself of the important things of your life.

Then twice a year or so reevaluate priorities again. You will find your way out of the maze, the obstacle.

Then you will find time for communication with God.

3

How-to: Finding Time

The alarm sounds. It's another day.

What do you have to do before you can face the morning? Shower? Drink a cup of coffee?

Many people don't even feel very Christian until they've had a cup of coffee to start the day.

George Mueller—greatly used of God in the early 1830s to initiate a project for the housing and care of orphans in the city of Bristol, England—considered his first responsibility in the morning was to nourish his soul.

We, too, need to take the responsibility for our souls' nourishment by finding the right time for communicating with God.

Here are ways to help in scheduling time for God.

Create time

If we think of this as an appointment with God, we'll set aside time to spend with the Lord like we do for any other appointment.

If we give ourselves all day, we'll take all day and possibly never do it. First thing in the morning is best, but may not always be possible. Become innovative in finding other time spans: coffee break, when waiting for someone, getting up earlier.

Many can rightfully say, "I don't have time."

We all have the same amount of time. It's how we choose to use it.

There is time enough, but there is not too much time. Someone said, "There is no need for rushed haste, but there is no room for waste."

To prove this to yourself, you might enjoy logging your time for twenty-four hours. When I did this, the results surprised me. I discovered I always find time for what is important to me.

Say, "Yes," to God in the morning. Just as we say yes to getting up, getting dressed, eating breakfast, or going to work. Not saying yes brings failure because it breaks the relationship, the bond between the soul and God.

We take time to read books, magazines, and newspapers. When periodicals come to our homes, we feel obligated to scan them at least, because we paid for them and don't want to waste money. As Christians we are obligated to know what God has to say to us after all He has done for us.

In an advertising campaign, a Seattle newspaper asked people to vow to read their paper every morning. Many people gave testimonials of how they couldn't start their day without it, because they believed in and needed this newspaper.

Some of us think we can sit back, and God will miraculously fill us with wisdom. Years later we'll still be waiting, because we have to make the first step. We have to become involved now, not tomorrow.

Now is the time

Now is the time to make the choice. Now is the time for communication with God.

Recently I heard of a young man who thought he had plenty of time. He told his pastor six years ago he planned to make some positive changes in his life and live for the Lord. Nothing changed though, because he only talked about it rather than taking some kind of action.

Six years passed...he is out of a job. He is out of a marriage. Life is passing.

He thought he could drift.

The Christian life is either up or down. There are no plateaus. "Plateaus" are only illusions that deceive us in to thinking we can coast. In reality, flat ground goes up or down gradually with the curvature of the earth, depending upon which direction we're going.

If we feel lulled into thinking we're fine, it's because we're descending so slowly we don't notice.

If we're striving, our life is on the upward slant. This is making choices for change.

Change is not comfortable. It makes us uncertain and uneasy. Who knows how it will work out in the end?

Yet, change is essential to growth. All the little choices change the course of the rest of our lives. Great things are connected by many small things.

Choice is the nonverbal communication that sets the basis for true communion with God.

Communication with God is a decision. Decide to communicate no matter what.

Write down the time

When I plan communicating with God, I am more likely to stay with it if I write down my goals.

To record your time at the beginning of each week use an index card, date book, journal, or electronic device. The time you set does not need to be the same hour every day; it may vary. Use the time that works for you.

Schedule a few minutes a day

The reason I suggest a few minutes is because this is much more realistic for life's busy schedules. It sounds great to say, "Spend an hour a day with the Lord," but how many can consistently do it. So it's better to spend a few minutes a day regularly. This gives steadiness.

Schedule this time for five days a week. Most of us have disruptive schedules on the weekend. There is no sense in making something as enjoyable as communication with God drudgery. So on the weekends think about what was learned that week, on occasion, and let it go at that.

Take one minute now to fill in the time for communication with God for the next five days.

All you have to do is devote just minutes a day. You will see a marked change in your relationships with others and with God. Each minute of effort brings maximum results.

Once you establish this habit, you'll get the benefit—survival.

Choosing God Minute Manager
(Take a minute to decide)

Write down your time for each day:
(It can be the same everyday or different times.)

    Day 1_____
    Day 2_____
    Day 3_____
    Day 4_____
    Day 5_____

4

Benefit: Survival

Some years ago Ron and I resigned our church in the Seattle area to start traveling in ministry. We searched for a house in the South Dakota Black Hills—in the shadow of Mount Rushmore—as a retreat to come home to. After looking four different times, we finally found our "retreat." We enjoyed watching the wild life and the splendor of nature every day.

One misty June morning after we moved in, I looked out our living room window to witness a miracle: brand-new, spotted fawns trying to walk on wobbly legs. All summer I watched in wonder at the antics of these twin fawns. It seemed one of them always strayed from the mother only to bawl in distress when mother was out of sight. Then his parent responded in answer to the distressed baby, and the fawn leaped over to mom. The moment of panic passed.

Why did this fawn need its mother? She was his food source. To this little fawn, she was survival.

Like this fawn, if we don't get the nutrition we need, we will die slowly. Starvation is serious. Often we read about and see emaciated people of the world in news stories. We feel deep sorrow. We should, because the situation is appalling. It's unforgettable. These people don't have any choice in the matter.

Spiritually we have a choice. We choose to starve without the Bible or survive with the Bible. Some may say, "It takes discipline to read the Bible every day."

This is spiritual food. Does it take discipline to eat food for the physical body?

The answer is no, of course not. It takes discipline not to eat. Ask anyone who has been on a diet.

Yet, just because we know the Bible well and even know the Bible as our source, we still tend to search for spiritual food and survival from places unrelated to God or His Word.

A friend told me about his struggle to keep up his physique. He walked into a bookstore and picked up an attractive book that promised flat abs in thirty days to help him stay in great physical shape. It sounded good.

Paul (not his real name) bought the book and took it home. He almost memorized it.

The next morning, excited about the prospect of a new look, Paul started the routine. Up, down, one, two, three, four. Over and over he doggedly performed the exercises every morning. He even cut time with God short to pursue this promising new venture.

After two weeks of this, Paul's muscles hurt. He continued for the whole month. On the morning of the thirtieth day he bounded out of bed anticipating his new image and rushed to the full-length mirror.

"Let's see...well...maybe if I squint. What's the use. There's very little change." Paul was disappointed!

In perspective, exercise is needful. The facts are: We can be caught up in vanities and push God aside.

You'd think we'd learn, but occasionally it's like someone said, "I still fall for the promises of strangers who give seminars and write books to make me richer, thinner, and happier. Somehow I never become richer, thinner, happier, or anything else for that matter."

The real riches, the answers to life's problems, true happiness, and spiritual survival dwell in Christ, in taking time for communication with God through his Word.

I believe all of us want spiritual survival. It takes positive choices. Communication with God will never disappoint us, and it gives us the spiritual food and strength we need to survive. In the end, it's more than survival.

It is winning every day.

Part Two: Loving God

"To see Your strength and Your glory." Psalm 63:2

5

Obstacle: Selecting Memories

The Bible says we are to love the Lord our God with all our hearts, with all our souls, and with all our minds.

So why does loving God seem so difficult? What holds us back?

Our memories.

Day after day we select and store negative happenings of our lives and go over those events in our thoughts and in words to others until those negatives are long past. Our private worlds then become combat zones. The past rages with the present until the past takes over. When past, negative memories control the present, it makes it harder and harder to love God or others in the present.

Every day is a gift. Often that gift is forfeited when built-up negatives of the past destroy pleasure of the present and opportunities of the future.

Someone said, "Our present is decided by our response to our past and our future is decided by our present response."

We all have a tendency toward the negative. Just notice our mouths. When we're not smiling, the corners turn down. When we make the effort, the corners turn up.

Winning the battle over building up negative memories can be conquered by learning the skills of forgetting.

Identify what needs to be forgotten. There are two categories I will cover in this chapter: false expectations and offenses. These are the two areas I experienced and observe that most of people have difficulty dealing with and putting behind.

False expectations

False expectations are conjured-up outcomes—when we expect results in response to our preconceived arrangements.

Bob and Mary (not their real names) decided to go into business. They didn't consult God or ask his advice; they went ahead with their plans. They bought the right equipment, advertised in the right places, and decided their goals. When God didn't meet their expectations—their venture failed—Mary told a friend. "We didn't deserve that from God. He didn't come through for us."

This couple made the mistake many of us do: they tried using God instead of loving and seeking God. This is immature love.

Immature love thinks of God as one who satisfies their needs and wants and says, "I love God because I need God."

Mature love says, "I need God because I love God."

We also can set up false expectations for spouse, children, friends, Christian leaders, churches, and jobs.

Because we live in a society where everyone's expectations are that everything will be and should be perfect, when our false expectations aren't realized, we become discouraged.

I heard a minister say, "Discouragement is the illegitimate child of false expectations."

Discouragement leads to selecting resentments for our memories and breaks down communication with God. So let's discontinue false expectations.

Let God be God.

Let those around us be who they are.

Now let's look at the other negative that keeps us from communication with God.

Offenses

Offenses are the hurts we acquire from the things people say or do against us. Paul Y. Cho wrote, "Those things people do for us are written on water, quickly disappearing. However, those things people do against us are written in tablets of stone, often remembered."

How true that saying is. We tend to remember the bad and forget the good. It's so typical of us to forget the benefits of life and remember the offenses and secretly or vocally blame those persons involved for our current misery.

Sometimes we even blame God for allowing these offenses that control our behavior for a lifetime.

Here's an example of a frivolous incident—but it gets my point across—that occurred when I was attending college.

One of my girl friends said to me one day, "LaVonne, if you'd wear a different kind of hose, your legs would look better. You'd get more dates."

I was flabbergasted. I did think about her comment for a while and decided not to take her advice. I just went on with my life as usual.

It so happened that I married the young man she had her eye on, and I've lived happily every after.

Thirty years later I spoke at a retreat in San Diego, California. After a morning session, a former Miss South Dakota came up to me and said, "LaVonne, you have the most beautiful legs I have ever seen. I judge beauty contests and I know good-looking legs. I couldn't get past watching your legs to hear what you were saying."

Right then I laughed aloud because my college friend's comments of so many years ago flashed into my mind. I compared her words with the comments of this beauty queen. As I compared the two remarks, I was glad I hadn't let my college friend's words control my life.

Learning from that incident, I now say:

Get a second opinion!

There are good reasons why one person's or a small group of persons' hurtful and painful words or actions cannot direct our lives.

First, it's just one person's or small group of persons' opinions or deeds.

Second, we need to forget the past—leave it all behind, let go of it all. Because if we don't let go of it, that event or that person will control our lives for the rest of our lives. However, when hurts and pain are deep, forgetting will take some extra effort.

Life is what is happening now, not what happened in the past. We can forget all of those negatives—false expectations and offenses—with an effective plan for forgetting.

Practicing Forgetting Guide

1. Ask forgiveness of God and others for anything you might have said or done. Ask God to forgive you for expecting what He never intended and to remove all bitterness and resentments.

Make a list of individuals you may have hurt by your false expectations or offenses. Then ask their forgiveness with a phone call, letter, or visit. Tear up the list. Throw away the pieces. Work on forgetting the past. Don't forget to forgive yourself for all past mistakes.

"If we confess our sins, he is faithful and just to forgive us our sins and to cleanse us." I John 1:9

God gives us a clean page to start over.

2. Forgive those who offended you. Rehearsing the words and deeds in your mind and telling others what was said or done is not forgiving. This keeps you blaming others for your unhappiness and extends the time of pain and sorrow.

Jesus instructed the disciples, "If you have anything against anyone, forgive him, that your Father in heaven may also forgive you your trespasses." Mark 11:25

3. Practice forgetting. Technically, I know it's not possible to forget, because events and thoughts do remain in our subconscious mind. But we can practice forgetting.

This is the key: Take the responsibility to replace any thoughts of false expectations and past offenses when they come to mind with a scripture verse. Any verse of your choice will do, but a good verse to use is Philippians 4:8.

> "Whatever things are true, whatever things are noble, whatever things are just, whatever things are pure, whatever things are lovely, whatever things are of good report, if there is any virtue and if there is anything praiseworthy…meditate on these things."

Verse nine goes on to tell us we are to put into practice all we've learned. It's our choice. The Word of God has power to heal our memories and deep hurts.

On the first day you practice forgetting you may have to replace those negative-happening thoughts with scripture verses fifty times. The next day it might be only forty times. The third day, twenty times. By the end of a month thoughts of false expectations and offenses will be pushed far to the back of your mind, and you will be on your way to practicing forgetting successfully.

You can only think one thought at a time. Make it a good one!

Whenever new offenses or false expectations occur, use the above three steps. Be very selective about what you store in your memory. Shake off false expectations and offenses when they occur like dogs shake water off their backs.

One day after teaching my Practicing Forgetting Plan in a seminar, a gentleman who attended approached me and said,

"LaVonne, my kids have said and done many hurtful things recently. If I just throw their words and actions off like a dog shakes off water, isn't that hardhearted?"

I replied, "No. It's survival."

Disappointments, hurtful comments, and ugly deeds are too heavy to carry through a lifetime. By practicing forgetting the pain lessens in time. God's Word brings eventual healing.

Selective memories can be like a favorite photo album with only the good pictures and favorite times included.

6

How-to: Focusing on God

God made us to love Him. I believe that most of us want to become involved with God in a deeper way, because we need expression for our souls.

As a musician needs freedom to express musical talent and a writer strives for an outlet of articulated thoughts, a human being yearns to communicate love for God, the Creator.

Loving God is: focusing on who God is in a quiet place with a plan in mind.

Loving God

To love God is to know God. Loving God takes time and knowledge to adore and worship Him. The reason God made humankind in His image was that we might worship and adore Him.

Anyone who worships God and desires to understand the greatness of God must exclude worship of anyone or anything else. It is not sufficient to view Him from a remote and detached viewpoint. We need intimate contact with Him to develop any genuine respect or grasp his awesomeness.

The key to developing a warm relationship with God is by loving and adoring Him. This comes from the heart—forgetting comfortable ideas of God, surrendering desires, giving without intent of receiving, coming as children and servants, and realizing that God doesn't see one as better than the other.

The place

As the time you have chosen for communication with God—discussed in Chapter 3—arrives, quiet your mind. Empty it of cares and distractions by concentrating on loving God. Reject every interruption within your power. If necessary, turn off your phone and kill the buzzing fly. Get rid of as many distractions as possible. Learn to block out noises.

Find a special place—your own sanctuary—for communicating with God. It can be your bedroom, a certain chair in the living room, garden, or patio. Be sure it's right for you and conducive for worship and communication.

After you decide upon your sanctuary, gather any materials you desire—your favorite Bible and Bible translations, journal or index cards or electronic device, and dictionary.

Place all the supplies you have chosen in your place of sanctuary to make communicating convenient for you.

The daily guide

Often we don't take time to love the Lord because we don't know how. Worship can be frustrated by our lack of words and phrases. If we are to love, adore and worship God and Christ with the aid of the Holy Spirit—what do we say and what do we do?

In the following daily guide, every time we communicate with God we start by loving Him in words, Scripture, song, or expression of our souls—a different focus for every day of the optional, five-day plan for loving God. I suggest you spend about two to five minutes a day on this focus.

Day 1: Focus on one characteristic of God

The level of worship will be determined by the conception of the one I worship. The only thing I have to compare God to is myself or another human being. He is so great; I cannot comprehend Him considering just humanness. So I must use terms that describe God.

A. W. Tozer explains God exceptionally well in his book *The Knowledge of the Holy*. On the next page I list the attributes of God—attributes meaning character traits correctly ascribed to God—he discusses for focusing on who God is. Here is a list to help you focus on who God is.

To make this a deeper experience, you can look up each characteristic in the dictionary. Then use your own words and thoughts to probe the depths of God's character. Words to describe Him can never be exhausted. It will take an eternity of loving to understand completely who He is. This is the beginning of comprehension.

Attributes of God

Self-existent: God has no origin, He is self-dependent.

Self-sufficient: God is what He is in Himself, the I Am.

Eternal: God is unending in existence.

Infinite: God is limitless, measureless.

Immutable: God never changes. God is not developing.

Omniscient: God is all wise.

Omnipotent: God is all powerful.

Omnipresent: God is present everywhere.

Transcendent: God is exalted over all, none like Him.

Faithful: God never fails.

Good: God bestows us with blessings everyday.

Just: God guarantees safety to all who put trust in Him.

Mercy: Because of God's mercies we are not consumed.

Grace: God grants us undeserved favor.

Love: God is our friend. He first loved us.

Holy: God's holiness is complete order, nothing lacking.

Sovereign: God is free to do whatever He wills.

Day 2: Focus on one name of Christ, Son of God

Human categories are not adequate to describe Christ, but the Bible is rich with names—over 350—that define and declare our Lord. One option during this time is to look up each name in the dictionary to assist you with more insight and deeper thought. Then, if you wish, express some of those thoughts aloud to help clarify thoughts of Christ. You'll discover it's a privilege to bless the Lord.

I composed an alphabetized list of names of Christ to help you get started focusing on Jesus Christ. Add some of your own favorite names of Christ to the list.

Names of Christ

Advocate, Alpha, Anointed One, Apostle, Author
Beginning, Beloved, Bread of life, Bridegroom
Captain, Chief Cornerstone, Christ, Counselor, Creator
Dayspring, Daystar, Defender, Deliverer, Door
Elect, Ensign, Eternal Life, Everlasting Father
Faithful Witness, Finisher of our Faith, Friend
Gift of God, Glorious Lord, Good Shepherd, Guide
Head of the Church, Healer, High Priest, Holy One, Hope
I Am, Intercessor, Inheritance, Immanuel, Immortal
Jehovah-Jireh, Jesus, Judah, Judge, Just One
King, King Everlasting, King of Glory, King of Kings
Lamb of God, Life, Light, Lion of Judah, Lord of Glory
Master, Mercy Seat, Messenger, Messiah, Mighty God
Name above Every Name, Never-failing Guide, Nazarene
Offering, Omega, Overcomer
Physician, Priest, Prophet, Prince of Peace
Quest of my Soul, Quiet Place
Redeemer, Refiner, Refuge, Resurrection, Righteousness
Savior, Shepherd, Son of God, Son of Man
Teacher, Temple, Treasure, Tree of Life, Truth
Very Present Help in Time of Trouble, Vine
Way, Witness, Word, Wonderful Counselor, Worthy

Day 3: Focus on the Holy Spirit

Invite the Holy Spirit into your life to guide you into all Truth, to comfort you, and to lead you.

You might say, "Come, Holy Spirit, I need you," as an invitation to Him.

Day 4: Read a psalm aloud

Every time you read something aloud, the vocal cords and the ears make a double impression on your mind. Choose five to ten verses of a favorite psalm or a psalm that articulates the attributes of God. To get you started, you can begin with Psalm 1 and go from there. Read each psalm with energy, feel the energy of God in your spirit, and concentrate on the statements that focus on the character of God or give praise to the Lord.

Day 5: Express your love to Him

This can be done orally, in thought, or in song. Love Him for who He is, rather than for what He has done.

Try to make this fresh. Avoid repeating old thoughts and worshiping the Lord from memory.

At times there will be no adequate words to express what you feel. God is so awesome, you can't speak. In those moments, sit before Him in the quietness of heart where words aren't necessary.

When this second aspect of communication with God becomes part of you, you will find expression for your soul and will sense a deep security in the Lord.

Loving God Minute Manager
(Allow two to five minutes each day.)

Day 1: Focus on one characteristic of God.
Day 2: Focus on one name of Christ.
Day 3: Focus on the Holy Spirit.
Day 4: Read a psalm aloud.
Day 5: Express your love to Him.

7

Benefit: Security

On a balmy, August day the seven children of Dr. Gertrude Tosten took their deceased, eighty-nine-year-old mother to Cresco, a northeastern Iowa town, and laid her to rest beside her husband, Dr. A. B. Tosten. As the fifth child of these parents, memories of their love, their teachings, and their examples rushed back to me as I stood with the others in the Oak Lawn Cemetery paying them tribute. What a heritage they left us.

Later our caravan of families explored familiar streets past the school, the library, and downtown near the grey stucco church on the corner. My home town had changed little in twenty-six years since I walked those sidewalks. It appeared Cresco was out to impress me. Houses gleamed in top repair, and lawns aired recent manicures. It looked better than I remembered. Ah, what a haven.

Near the edge of town, we stopped by the house we had lived in: a two-story, white house with a front porch. It was much the same, except now the living room extended out twenty feet with a deck added onto the back. The inside, no doubt, changed with each new owner, but the front stairway with its two landings probably remains the same.

Sitting in the car in front of the house, I thought about two pictures that hung above the first landing of that stairway when we lived there. I remembered how I sat on the steps and put myself in those scenes.

One portrayed *Jesus as Shepherd* with his sheep gathered around his feet while He nestled a lamb. As I gazed at that portrayal, I became the lamb cuddled to the Savior. I could feel his arms about me.

The other was *The Guardian Angel* depicting two children crossing a rickety bridge spanning a raging creek with a guardian angel to guide them through the threatening storm. In my imaginings, my sister Jeanette and I were the children that walked the bridge while the angel hovered and protected us, even though the waters roared, the rain distorted sight, and the bridge creaked.

In both cases I felt safe.

My parents' love, my home town, and my family home decorated with vivid pictures brought security then. Now, all that is in the past. The security that remains—dad and mother's instructions (around the dining room table) to us children about the lasting security we possess and the sense of Christ's presence when we focus on loving God in Christ.

Safety

God provides a sanctuary beyond the pressures of life and supplies inspiration essential for the Spirit to help us carry on. He calls out to anyone who feels restricted by humanness, who wants contact with all wisdom, all power—something beyond self, family, career, or possessions. This place provides security that only God gives.

His presence

It's moving into His presence. Feeling security when comprehending who He is by focusing upon Him—His power, wisdom, presence, love, faithfulness, goodness, holiness, just to name a few characteristics from Chapter 6. Because security is a matter of the mind, when we choose to think upon God we will have security. In loving God, we become more aware of his presence.

This fellowship, this presence brings a snug feeling that the heart perceives. Security, despite what happens to us outwardly.

A few years ago, I experienced extreme frustration. I had sailed into a calm. At best, life's progress was in very slow motion. Nothing was happening.

When I chose to enter God's realm—God's presence by thinking upon the attributes of God, particularly the sovereignty of God—I realized God had my life in His hands. He does all things well.

If God finds pleasure in the circumstances of my life at any stage of my life, then I can rest in that and continue loving Him. Because in loving Him, it is important to me that I please God, not that I understand all that happens.

None of us ever wants to lose the sense of His presence through subtle misunderstanding or inattention.

Someone said, "Loving is costly, but the cost of not loving is even greater."

In loving Him, we find the security we need.

Part Three: Conversing with God

"I meditate on You in the night watches." Psalm 63:6

8

Obstacle: Listening to God

I watched a man on a television program describe how he depended on television ministers to interpret the Bible for him. When problems began to surface in these ministers' lives, this man lost faith. He told the emcee, "Now I'm agnostic."

Regardless of how well-known or famous someone is, what they have to say is not as important as what God has to say. The best way we can find out what God is saying is to listen to the voice of God.

William Gladstone said, "My only hope for the world is in bringing the human mind into contact with divine revelation."

It is the only way we can get through life successfully, to win.

Today each of us needs to hear from God for healing from hurts, direction for today, guidance for the future, wisdom for our families, strength for today, and a multitude of other reasons.

One man said, "Our trouble is not that God does not speak, but that we don't listen enough."

To listen means to heed or pay attention to what is said. We spend 80% of our waking hours communicating and 60% listening. We listen to spouse, children, friends, radio, television, but why not God? I believe there are obstacles that keep us from listening to God.

They are: finding peace, misinterpreting the Bible, and misunderstanding how God speaks.

Finding peace

There are three things that prevent us from finding peace: noise, talking, wrong attitudes.

Noise. In our noisy world peace is difficult. Still we need quiet to listen, because God's communications are often quiet. So to hear Him we have to turn up the quiet by tuning out or turning off distractions. Stay with the desire to listen to God.

Talking. The clatter of our own chatter can hinder our listening. We can be so busy talking we can't hear anything but the sound of our own voice.

Like the minister who went to prayer. He found he had nothing to say to the Lord, so he left the place of prayer. Later it occurred to him that he should have stayed and listened to what God had to say.

Wrong attitudes. Attitudes can destroy heart peace, and lack of peace restricts listening. God does not reveal truth when we are harboring bad attitudes. Pride and selfishness are examples of attitudes that keep us from properly understanding the Scriptures.

Finding peace is a choice.

I found I can move into and out of the range of God's voice. When I allow noises, distractions, and wrong attitudes that keep me from listening, I move out of the range of God's voice.

When peace reigns and I make myself available to Him, I move into the range of God's voice. Peace is mine as I decide what to focus my mind upon.

Peace becomes a reality by making right choices.

Misinterpreting the Bible

Is the Bible a rule book or a guide book? Those who believe it is a rule book and hold onto a misinterpretation of the Bible exhibit two harmful extremes: a reckless lifestyle or a legalistic approach.

A reckless lifestyle: This philosophy is that rules are made to be broken or stretch the rules and see how far one can go. Down in the hearts of these people, when they do wrong, they expect God to punish them. When God doesn't punish immediately upon wrong doing, they may begin to think there are no consequences. They continue on in a careless lifestyle without regarding themselves or others, not taking responsibility for the quality of their lives, and always looking for new escapes.

A legalistic approach: This philosophy has a rule for every aspect of life. If rules are broken, God is perceived as angry and unforgiving to anyone who may have broken one of those laws. Many people have been hurt by this ideology, because these people tend to be rude and pushy. Their behavior depicts God as a bully and unapproachable. They misinterpret the Bible. They cause others to develop hostile feelings toward God.

A guide book: Between the reckless lifestyle and the legalistic approach, triumphs the proper perception of the

Bible as a guide book. With this outlook markings are followed closely, so as not to get lost.

Above all, the Bible is not to be used as a rod to defeat people. The Bible is always by the side for quick reference and guidance.

There is a subtle difference between these two thoughts: the Bible as a rule book or as a guide book. The two are so vastly contrasted they never meet.

Choose to consider the Bible as a guide. It will make a big difference in quality of life.

Misunderstanding how God speaks

Over the years I have heard people define many different ways God spoke to them:

God speaks only through His Word.

God speaks through ministers and teachers.

God speaks with a still, small voice.

God speaks through experiences.

God speaks through visions and dreams.

So how does God speak? In reality, He speaks to all of us in all the above ways. Because we are all different, God speaks to us by different methods. Individually, we may not experience all His ways of speaking in our own lives because of how individual brains function.

It has to do with which side of our brain is most dominant: left-brain, right-brain, or balanced-brain. This puts us into three different categories of brain dominance with varying degrees of dominance in each category.

As I have studied this, I realized brain dominance has everything to do with the way I listen to God. The reason I hear God differently from another person is because of my particular brain dominance. Brain dominance affects all communication with God.

Researchers write that there are certain characteristics for the left-brain dominant person, the right-brain dominant person and the balanced-brain dominant person.

Brain-dominance traits

Left-brain dominant persons are: dependent on intellect, occupied by thoughts, word-oriented, analytical, deliberate, logical, verbal, practical, and disciplined. They listen to God with their intellect. Some of their occupations are scientists, writers, lawyers, speakers, and computer experts.

Right-brain dominant persons are: experience-oriented, prone to depression, see pictures and visions, emotional, instinctive, nonverbal, creative and free-spirited. They listen to God with their emotions. Some of their occupations are musicians, artists, composers and athletes.

Balanced-brain dominant persons are: a combination of both the left and right brain, in the middle, and a bit of both. They listen to God with both the intellect and the emotions. They often are editors, gallery owners, politicians, and sales persons.

To discover your brain dominance you may wish to take a few minutes to look over the following statements compiled by professional educators. Of each of the two statements, one is more likely to be chosen by a left-brained person and the other by a right-brained person. Place a mark by the A or B sentence that is characteristic of you.

Left-Brain, Right-Brain Dominance Evaluation

1.
A. I'm a tense person; I worry about getting things right.
B. I'm relaxed and easygoing; I don't fight life.

2.
A. I get depressed a lot.
B. I very seldom get depressed.

3.
A. When I learn something new, I flounder around until I get it. I never read directions.
B. When I learn something new, I work gradually and always follow directions.

4.
A. If I were in college, I would select art rather than math.
B. If I were in college, I would select math rather than art.

5.
A. I'm a deliberate shopper; I think about something before I buy it.
B. I'm an impulsive buyer; when I want something, I buy it.

6.
A. I often have hunches.
B. I don't trust hunches.

7.

A. I often have trouble putting my feelings and opinions into words.

B. I seldom have trouble putting my feelings and opinions into words.

8.
A. I am a better-than-average athlete.
B. I am not a very good athlete.

9.
A. When I parallel park a car, I usually have to pull out at least once and try another time.
B. When I parallel park a car, I usually get it right the first time.

10.
A. If I could choose, I would read a book rather than see a movie.
B. If I could choose, I would see a movie rather than read a book.

Now check your answers against this key, and then add up your total number of left and right responses.

1. A. Left, B. Right

2. A. Right, B. Left

3. A. Right, B. Left

4. A. Left, B. Right

5. A. Left, B. Right

6. A. Right, B. Left

7. A. Right, B. Left

8. A. Right, B. Left

9. A. Left, B. Right

10. A. Left B. Right

If you chose seven or more Left answers, you are probably left-brain dominant. If you chose seven or more Right answers, you are most likely right-brain dominant. If you ended up with a relative balance between Left and Right, you are in the middle group called balanced-brain.

Of course, this is not all-comprehensive, but it gives some indication of brain dominance.

The discovery of brain dominance is important because it helps to understand how God speaks to our conscious mind.

For example, the left-brain dominant person most often hears from the Lord by the Word of God, ministers and teachers, and a still small voice.

The right-brain dominant person most often hears from the Lord by mind-pictures of the Word, visions, and experiences.

The balanced-brain dominant person may hear from God in all the above ways at some time or other when God speaks to them.

Because God speaks to different people in different ways, this gives clearer understanding of God's ways of communicating.

We all benefit when we understand how God speaks and are careful to listen to Him when He does speak.

9

How-to: Responding

In conversation there are two elements: listening and responding. Once we work our way through the obstacle of listening to God, we are ready for responding to God.

It's easy to develop simple response skills by using this five-day guide in this chapter for responding and listening to God through the Bible.

Response skills

We respond to God when reading the Bible. This can be done literally from any location in the Bible by using whatever translation you are comfortable with.

This process is very personal and meaningful to you alone. Here are these helps to make the scriptures real for your personal life:

Ask God to direct you to the chapter or book of the Bible that will be most appropriate for you presently. Recognize God's Word as the propelling force of your life. When you are through with one chapter or book, ask the Lord to direct you to another chapter or book.

Relax and be yourself in His presence. Let Him come speak to you and then respond.

Tune in. Concentrate. Listen carefully. Forget yourself and anything else for the moment.

When my son Timothy talked to me while I was doing something else and thought I wasn't paying any attention, he'd take my face in both hands and make me look at him—right into his eyes. Then he had full eye contact, and he was satisfied. That is like concentration. Everything else is unimportant for the moment.

Response guide

If you have my book *Successful Living: Memorizing and Meditating*—formerly *Memorize and Meditate*—and follow that plan, continue to use that plan rather than the five-day guide on the next few pages. *Successful Living* is enhanced, however, by using all the other steps—choosing, loving, asking, winning—along with it. Just insert *Successful Living* into the Conversing with God part of this book.

Getting into the Bible every day is like working a crossword puzzle. The first time you look at a puzzle you know some of the words immediately. Then you leave the puzzle and come back to it. You see more words to fill in. Each time you look at the puzzle you see new solutions.

So it is with the verses you choose to read and meditate on, the first day you read the verses you get some good thoughts. Every day as you go back to the same verses you perceive new things you hadn't noticed before. You learn something new every day. This puts vitality and excitement into your devotional life. Below is the optional, five-day guide for conversing.

Day 1: Read Bible and think about verses

After you have selected your chapter or book, start at the beginning of a chapter and read 4-12 verses only. Read and think about the same group of verses every day the first week. The second week read another group of verses. Make breaks in groups of verses according to breaks in thought.

For instance, if you start in the book of John, begin by reading verses 1-5 every day for the first week. The second week read verses 6-13 every day. The third week read verses 14-18 every day. These divisions are following the New King James sections of thought. In your Bible this may be different so follow the breaks indicated.

You may choose to use index cards, journal, or electronic device. In case you opt for cards write John 1:1-5 on your cards the first week. Then carry those index cards, journal or electronic device with you and record your thoughts, feelings, and word meanings anytime during the week.

Options for new thoughts

Look beyond the superficial facts. As you read, focus on things you've never noticed before.

Create the scene. Notice the people, the place, and put yourself in the scene when it is possible. Use your five senses: hear, see, smell, feel, touch.

Focus on the main points. In John 1:1-5 some of the main points are: the Word is God, Jesus is life, He is light.

Day 2: Read Bible and look up words

Read your selected verses and notice a word or words. Take note of any words that stand out to you as you read.

Options for new thoughts

Look up words in the scripture text you are curious about. Look them up in an ordinary dictionary. It is rewarding to take time to discover meanings of words you think you already know.

Write researched words and their meanings on your card, in your journal, or electronic gadget.

Take a few moments to think about the definition you discover. Personalize the word meaning. Take it to heart.

For example when John 10:10 was included in my reading one week, I was curious about the words "abundant" and "life." So in looking up the word life, I discovered one of the meanings for the word is: the ability to bounce back. The meaning for abundant is: many times. So I can put the two definitions together and conclude that the Lord will give me the ability to bounce back from devastating circumstances as many times as I need in my life.

Day 3: Read Bible and ask questions

Read your selected verses and ask questions. It takes a question to bring an answer. Primarily your questions will be key thoughts or feelings about the verses you just read.

Options for new thoughts

Move from the known to the unknown. Identify the things you know in the verses, and then begin to investigate the things you don't know. Things are hidden in the beginning only as a means to revelation.

Seek out truth, not theory, by asking questions. What questions do these verses inspire? Boldly ask the questions that come to your mind. This is your opportunity to speak hidden questions to the Lord. Note a key verse, a leading lesson, a promise or an instruction.

What feelings, positive or negative, do these verses produce? Tell the Lord what you think or feel. Share what's in your heart with Him. You may desire to write some of your thoughts.

Day 4: Read Bible and listen to God

Read your selected verses and let the Holy Spirit open your mind to truth and application.

Options for new thoughts

Your most important moments before God are in your silence, your listening. Let your mind go in reflection of the verses. God will speak to you in words or pictures. It is all right to let your mind wander to other thoughts at this time. He may be trying to show you how to apply Scripture.

Listen with your mind. Try not to interrupt God or finish His sentence for Him or assume you already know what He is going to say. You don't need to respond.

An ancient Proverb says, "The most difficult thing of all is to keep quiet and listen."

Listen with your heart. Follow closely.

Consider that in communication experts tell us there are six elements that occur:

1. What was actually said
2. What you think was said
3. What was meant by what was said
4. What you actually heard
5. What you think you heard
6. What you think was meant by what you heard

Keep all of this in mind when you listen to God through the Word. Be sure you hear what God is saying through the verses of scripture you are reading.

Day 5: Read Bible and summarize

Read your selected verses.

Options for new thoughts

Express aloud thoughts and feelings. Capsulize. Discuss the scriptures with spouse, family, or friends.

Express by thinking of or drawing a picture. Share your feelings about the weekly verses with others

During the day think about what you heard from God. Then on the weekend let your mind go back to the verses of scripture and think about or picture them.

Feel the love.

Conversing with God Minute Manager

(Allow four to five minutes a day.)

Day 1: Read Bible and think about verses.
Day 2: Read Bible and look up words.
Day 3: Read Bible and ask questions.
Day 4: Read Bible and listen to God.
Day 5: Read Bible and summarize.

10

Benefit: Love

Seven-year-old Bill was playing by himself. He was completely lost in his own world, shooting baskets and perfecting his aim. He was immersed in his quest of skills. The neighbor girl Mary Lou came over to talk.

"Why did you come over? I was having fun until you came," quipped Bill.

Mary Lou began to cry. Now Bill didn't mean to hurt Mary Lou. He was just declaring the I-call-it-like-I-see-it communication of a child. He didn't mean to hurt as much as he intended to tell exactly how he felt. He had not yet matured to the point of knowing the importance of tactful conversation.

All of us have experienced the loneliness of rejection that Mary Lou felt when Bill rejected her. This story strikes at the heart of most of us because we need significant relationships and reassuring conversations. Times when loved ones or friends don't want us around or refuse to talk because of anger can be devastating. Feelings and thoughts of not being loved become predominant and affect every aspect of our lives.

It is also important for us to feel and know we are loved by God. Sensing God's love becomes a reality upon recognition of the voice of God and through that reassuring voice, sense God's love everyday in our lives.

Recognize the voice of God

When we know God and love Him, we will know His voice. We don't have to live in fear of not being able to recognize or hear His voice, but we do need to be aware of the voices we don't want to take over our minds and consequently our lives.

You may be thinking, *How can I recognize God's voice? How can I know if the voice I hear in my mind is the voice of God?*

The different voices that meander in and out of the passageways of our minds can be confusing. As I say for every spiritual exercise in this book, let's simplify our thoughts on this matter.

There are three voices in our minds. Here are their basic definitions:

Personal voice. This is the personal human thoughts of tasks, ideas, instruction, opinions, attitudes, and everyday activities. These are normal, everyday thoughts. If any of your personal thoughts destroy your peace, throw them out and think upon a verse of scripture. This will restore balance and serenity to your mind.

Evil-dart voice. These thoughts come in as unexpected darts and immediately cause confusion and loss of peace. They are accusatory, negative, hateful, lies, and wrong doing. There is no need to fear if you keep your mind focused; these dart thoughts cannot take over your mind unless you allow them to. If dart thoughts get you down, accuse you and generally defeat you, immediately choose to throw out those thoughts, and focus on a scripture verse.

God's voice. This is a quiet voice that is always encouraging, hopeful, instructive, positive, gentle in correction, victorious, triumphant, creative, and filled with love. Learn to listen to this voice carefully, and think on God's thoughts—the scriptures—at every opportunity throughout the day. When you first wake up in the morning, think about your weekly verses of scripture and listen to His before any other voices. When you lie down on your bed at night to sleep, think about the verses of scripture again. Your day will go better, and you will sleep better.

Sense God's love

God is love. God understands all languages and all cultures. His capacity to communicate is limitless. All people can successfully converse with God, and all of us need intimate conversation that gives us the sense of being loved and cherished.

What would happen if one day when you called upon God in desperation, "Lord, help me now!"

Instead of God's voice you hear an angel say, "One moment, please. Can you hold?"

Then an angel choir sings for you while you hold.

Impatient and irritated, you might say to yourself, "I called God. I don't need an angel choir. I need God."

Of course, this illustration is ridiculous. God is always there. He is there when we need someone to listen, someone to talk to, and someone to converse with.

Everyone needs someone to listen. Someone to hear all woes including sorrows, hurts, and inner feelings without fear of unfair judgment or rejection. One of the most disheartening things is to be misunderstood or be judged unfairly or rejected.

Everyone needs someone to talk to. We all have this basic need for talk and conversation. When we're alone we turn on the radio or television, talk to a pet, or sometimes to ourselves.

To help with this idea of conversation with the Lord, you might picture yourself and the Lord sitting in two easy chairs before a fireplace. The logs in the fireplace are crackling while the two of you involved in delightful conversation.

A left-brain dominant response will be the mental stimulation of deep conversation.

A right-brain response will be the supreme comfort of being in His presence — rest for the soul.

For all, it will be the satisfaction of inner, personal needs. Security in the fact that God loves you even more than you love Him.

You sense the reality of His love in intimate conversation.

Part Four: Asking of God

"Because You have been my help." Psalm 63:7

11

Obstacle: Praying

I heard a prayer seminar speaker say, "The average Christian spends only 90 seconds a day in prayer."

What is the reason for this? Is it possible we have apathetic feelings about prayer? Why does prayer seem to be one of the easiest rituals to break?

As I have analyzed this, I think there are many factors like schedules, distractions, and discouragement to name a few.

Another factor might be that in our society we are under the illusion if we have talked about it and read about it, we've done it. We love to talk about everything. Just look at how many talk shows are on radio and television and all the blogger sites on the Internet.

This philosophy carries over into our spiritual life and communication with God. We often talk about prayer and read about it, and think we have prayed. When in reality we haven't. Just talking about prayer dissipates the energy— perhaps even more, the enthusiasm—that would be channeled into doing. The more we talk, the less we want to pray. Then apathy thrives.

To create positive feelings for asking of God we need to define exactly what it is and understand that asking of God is part of our relationship with God. Asking is a natural outgrowth of loving God and conversing with God.

Bringing it down to fundamentals, prayer is simply petitions and intercessions that can require just a few minutes of our time every day. If our prayers do not change us, then we're not praying right.

Petitions

Petitions are requests for ourselves, asking for our personal needs. Ask for yourself before asking for others. There is no need to feel guilty about asking for yourself first. In John 17 Jesus prayed for himself first, then for his disciples, then for others.

Petitions guide

1. Ask forgiveness for any wrongs committed. Ask, "Have I done anything in the last 24 hours I'm ashamed of?" The Psalmist said if we have evil in our heart, the Lord will not hear us. We need forgiveness. This step of personal forgiveness is the condition to be met for prayer to be effective

2. Identify needs specifically. Learn to ask sentence requests as described in Chapter 12.

3. Ask with confidence. In Ephesians Paul tells us we have confidence by our faith in Him. God will direct our desires and thoughts when we converse with Him in the Word. He will direct our asking to conform to His will. This phenomenon of our will becoming His is sustained by communication with God.

Intercessions

The other kind of asking in the Bible is intercessions. This is asking God on behalf of others. It takes great selflessness to have interest in others when our own needs may be great. Yet it is always worth every effort. Look at Job 42:10.

> "And the Lord restored Job's losses when he prayed for his friends. Indeed the Lord gave Job twice as much as he had before."

Here are three things that will help in intercessory prayer. Keep in mind this is your daily asking time and is not including those times when God may call you to extensive intercession. That is another book in itself. Some may not get involved in intercessory prayer simply because they don't think they have time for it. Below is a pattern to use in your daily communicating with God, you'll find it won't take as much time as you may think.

Intercessions guide

1. Make a list of intercessions on a card or journal or electronic device. In Chapter 12 I give more information regarding this.

2. Ask in specific requests for all on the list. Use sentence requests explained in Chapter 12.

3. Ask immediately when a request comes to mind. Whether you are driving, shopping, or at work. When you think of a person or request on your list of intercessions, ask the Lord immediately.

This makes communication with God day and night a reality and brings immediate sense of purpose to your life.

Intercession is not a complex plan that happens and then just ends. Each person interconnects with and affects other persons in never-ending cycles around the world twenty-four seven. Prayer brings together the world.

12

How-to: Requesting

Sometimes we complicate prayer. This inhibits our spiritual life. As you read in the last chapter, there are two kinds of prayers—petitions and intercessions.

The how-to is simple. Keep prayer uncomplicated or we will begin to think we can't handle another complication. We can pray through quickly when we need to.

Pattern for Requests

Prayer can be puzzling. The disciples were puzzled about prayer and asked the Lord to show them how. It is simply bringing requests to the Lord with this form.

1. Begin by addressing God the Father. "Our Father who art in Heaven," was used by Jesus in the Lord's Prayer. Using this term is acknowledgment of God as Father and shows proper respect.

2. Ask sentence requests. Specific, sentence requests are the most effective. The more clarity, the better.

3. End with "In Jesus' Name." Jesus told the disciples that if they asked anything in His name, he would grant it.

Sentence Requests

Often short prayers are the most effective ones. Sentence requests are specific requests with the extras cut out. Still I know there are people who think prayers must be long and filled with flowery phrases. Like the following example:

> Heavenly Father, thou knowest Homo sapiens art but dust. Thou, in thine omniscience, discernest copious provocations and evil battalions to dissuade me. Eradicate mine infirmity. Amen. (Ah-men)

This sounds like a worthy prayer, but I think even God scratches His head over the above kind of prayer and wonders if that person even knows what was requested.

Let us not think because our prayers are short and to the point, they are not worthy. An indication of a healthy prayer life is when prayers are answered; not how flowery the speech or how many hours prayed.

Prayer is more practical when asked like this one:

> Heavenly Father, help me control my tongue today. In Jesus Name, Amen.

Immediately, you see the difference between the two prayers.

The business world has a word to describe the first prayer — gobbledygook. It means: excessive verbiage or wordiness that persons use to make their prayers sound more important than they really are.

Just like the toothpicks I carry with me. The manufacturer named them wooden inter-dental stimulators. They are only toothpicks. Nothing more and nothing less.

It's important to get to specifics in asking of God as I mentioned earlier. Specific prayers are sentence requests with the unnecessary words subtracted. Here is the one-minute key to forming sentence requests.

One-minute Sentence Requests

1. Ask the Lord how you should ask for each person or need on your list.
2. Listen to the next words or scripture verse you hear in your mind.
3. Write that request or verse on a card or journal or electronic notes.

This prayer or scripture verse God gives you then is the prayer you will offer for that person or need.

Go through each request using this method. Your prayers will be according to God's will, and you will see answers, because your prayers will be cooperating with the purposes of God.

Marie (not her real name) attended a Bible class when I taught about sentence requests. For years she prayed for her mother with no results. Let me tell you her story.

When Marie was five, her parents divorced. Her devastated mother started drinking, and soon she left Marie with her paternal grandparents to raise and then withdrew from life.

This hurt, lonely child could not understand how her mother could just give her away to someone else and not care. Marie grew up resenting and judging her mother.

Finally, she even hated her mother.

A handsome young man came into Marie's adult life. Marriage brought her happiness for a time. Then God blessed them with children.

But a thorn annoyed Marie—her mother. This thorny relationship with her mother began to affect her marriage. All contacts with her mother were not pleasant. Phone conversations always ended with conflict. Personal visits were out of the question.

In hurt and defeat Marie always prayed for her mother, "Lord, straighten up my mother. She's a mess."

After Bible class Marie went home and decided to follow my teaching about specific requests. She sat before the Lord and worshipped Him. Then with her Bible she began communication with God through the Word. When she came to the time for asking of God she prayed, "Lord, how should I pray for my mother?"

The next thoughts that came to her mind were: *Show me ways to love my mother.*

God changed her prayer completely from a negative prayer to a positive one.

With some misgivings Marie began to ask this new specific request regularly, "Show me ways to love my mother."

An idea developed: *Buy your mother a rose and take it to her.*

On New Year's Eve, Marie went to her mother's apartment. She knocked on the door. Her mother came and stood in the doorway. Marie shook as she handed her mother the rose and choked on the words, "I love you, Mother."

Puzzled by Marie's behavior, the mother took the rose and shut the door in her face.

Marie didn't give up. As she continued to pray, "Show me ways to love my mother," God gave ideas for many other gifts for her mother. Each time she delivered them she said, "I love you, Mother," before she left her apartment.

When Christmas arrived the next year, Marie invited her mother to join her family for Christmas—something she dreaded in previous years. Her mother accepted the invitation and they all enjoyed grandma with them.

The walls of separation crumbled in the lives of both Marie and her mother. Soon Marie's mother came back to the Lord, and she quit drinking. Now mother and daughter not only spend happy holidays together but treasure mother-daughter time frequently.

The restoration was complete, an answered sentence request.

Daily Guide for Requests

A daily guide is very helpful for asking of God. Since we live in a needy world, prayer can sometimes be overwhelming with so many requests.

In this fourth aspect for communication with God follow this optional, five-day plan, and you will be able to cover most of the requests on your list by remembering them once a week.

It will look something like this:

Day 1. personal requests
Day 2. spouse/children/family requests
Day 3. friends requests
Day 4. church requests
Day 5. world requests

Alter this to fit your needs. This plan just gives you an idea of how you can break down asking to fit your life and schedule.

You may desire to use index cards or journal or electronic notes to record all your requests and carry with you throughout the week. Put the date you begin asking, and most important put the date each request is answered.

Seeing evidence of answers before your eyes is an immense faith-builder. Gratefully praise and thank the Lord for answered prayer.

Options for personal requests

Include the full-range of your personal life. When requests are answered; then go on to others. Keep it simple with just a few requests at a time, because you can only work on one thing at a time.

Try praying the scriptures for yourself. God loves His Word. This blesses the Lord and will bless you.

Options for your family requests

Your immediate family requests. This includes your spouse, children, parents and all the other relatives. If you have a large family, you may need to take two days for this.

Look for solutions rather than focusing on the problems. Know this: God will keep spouse, children, parents, brothers, and sisters in His care.

Options for your friends requests

Friends need our prayers and support. You may also include neighbors on this day. Many do not know the Lord. Love and friendship can bring them to Christ. Use this day for family members if you have a large family.

Options for your church requests

List church, congregational, program needs, or financial needs of your church. When requests are made known take note of them and bring these requests to the Lord on this day. Also include some of the auxiliary programs, Sunday church, classes, and various meetings during the week. Pray for the pastors, their families and staff.

Options for your world requests

Requests can cover a broad range. They can cover your job, your city, your state, your country, leaders of your country, missionaries abroad, and the whole world. Of course, you can't possibly cover all these topics in one day, but you can choose a different one every week

Ask requests from the many excellent web sites that list prayer requests. Use some of these on your list.

Asking of God Minute Manager

(Allow two to five minutes a day)

Day 1: Make specific requests for yourself.

Day 2: Make specific requests for spouse/children/family.

Day 3: Make specific requests for your friends.

Day 4: Make specific requests for your church.

Day 5: Make specific requests for your world.

13

Benefit: Self-esteem

All of us can give examples of incidents in childhood that shattered our self-esteem. We all have unique, painful memories of childhood. The hurt of those memories may parallel being the last one chosen for team sports or worse, suffering physical or mental abuse.

Then we become adults and discover life doesn't shield us from affliction. The struggle for self-esteem can be lifelong.

Yet the Lord feels our hurt. He prizes each one of us, without exception. This means He highly esteems us and considers us important. He wants us to know this. To show His regard, God sent His Son, Jesus Christ, to give His life for us that we might live with Him eternally. He further demonstrates His love everyday when He grants our various requests. He specializes in the personal touch.

Answered prayer raises our self-esteem, as we recognize who God is and find our esteem in Christ. Then we continue to ask, seek and knock for other requests. But what about those times when we ask, seek, knock, and nothing occurs—the waiting times.

Ask, Seek, and Knock

Luke 11:9 says, "So I say to you, ask, and it will be given to you; seek, and you will find; knock, and it will be opened to you."

Ask means to crave and desire. We need not be afraid to ask the Lord for our needs and desires. If our desires are not of His will, He will gently change them in communication with God.

Seek literally means to seek and to worship God. In other words, to communicate with Him. That covers aspects two and three of communication with God: loving God and conversing with God.

Knock means to rap, not pound on the door or force it open. Because if we use our own pressure to open the doors in life we may experience three unfavorable circumstances:

1. Embarrassment: This is opening a door unexpectedly and suffering embarrassment over what is seen that was not supposed to be seen.

2. Hostility: In Seattle a robber forced his way into a private home. The resident was ready for him with a gun and shot the robber dead.

3. Nothing: When doors are opened too soon, there may be nothing, nothing after much work and manipulation.

Still it takes courage to continue to rap. You may wonder if your efforts are in vain.

The literal translation of Luke 11:9 is keep on asking, keep on seeking, keep on knocking. Regardless of how long it takes, one month, one year, five years, or twenty years. Wait for an answer.

Waiting for Answers

In the waiting process, we can get discouraged and hope fizzles. Perhaps hope doesn't wane all at once, but evaporates at a slow rate. One day it is gone, and we don't even notice. Then we quit hoping. Our confidence fizzles. We forget temporarily that God is immutable and omnipotent.

Here's some encouragement, if the answer is delayed, our self-esteem need not suffer with thoughts that God does not care anymore. Know that He sees and hears us the moment we send our request His way.

It takes continued trust and patience.

Our daughter Karen was a children's pastor for years in a great church in Seattle. One Sunday she asked the kids the meaning of patience. One little boy quickly retorted, "It's when you wait for a long, long, long time and don't get mad."

In the waiting for answers, our emotions can take control. Here are five emotional stages we meet with during the wait.

Enthusiasm: Specific, sentence requests are formulated. At the beginning, there is much hope and enthusiasm.

Faith: Self-talk is used to reinforce the spirit. We may say, "This is a great God. He said in the Bible He will answer. This mountain shall be removed."

Conflict: Thoughts become confused. *Was my sentence request right? Did the Lord even hear?*

Despair: These are dark days. You may think, "The answer is never coming. I might as well give up."

Bitterness or **acceptance**: A choice is made to embrace one belief or the other.

Bitterness: God didn't come through; God isn't fair.
Acceptance: God's will be done in His time and His way.

We can all make it through long times of asking by depending on what we know is right and remind ourselves to keep on asking, seeking, and knocking and remember that God does value and esteem us.

God can move any person, place, or thing to answer our requests.

He respects us and gives us self-esteem.

Part Five: Winning With God

"My soul follows close behind You." Psalm 63:8

14

Obstacle: Allowing Humanness

Life can be like groping for a shoe in the bottom of a dark closet—you hope it's going to be there. You hope you're going to make it.

Life can be like putting your fingers on the wrong keys on the keyboard. The word you type ends up looking like— eubbubg—instead of winning. For the winning combination just move the left hand over one key to the left and move the right hand over one key to the right.

For the winning combination in life let go of negative thinking that keeps you from winning and allow for your humanness.

Two of the primary, negative ideas that hinder winning are: perfectionism and number-one philosophy. When we let these go we can learn what winning really is.

Perfectionism

The problem with thinking I must be perfect, is that I can't live up to my own expectations. Then I continually think of myself as a failure.

The reality of life is our humanness. When we allow for this, it permits us to make mistakes. It moves us away from perfectionism and sets us free to grow and change.

Life doesn't always fall into neat patterns. It is a mix of ups and downs. Sometimes we're up. Sometimes we're down. Accept this. God doesn't ask us to perform Herculean feats. He uses both our strengths and our weaknesses.

Some are silenced because they maximize their faults and minimize their strengths. Don't expect more of yourself than God does. You can't be more than human. God's purpose is not that we be perfect, but be who we are.

God uses us as we are.

The Lord will help you fulfill your role in life. You do get better at living. No one gets worse and worse at anything. You get better and better with Christ. Don't waste your life trying to be perfect. Paul said, "For me to live is Christ."

Number-one philosophy

No one ever remembers who came in second. That's why there is this craving to be number one. We want to be remembered. We want it all. Is all enough? Does it satisfy?

This wanting to get ahead, this drive to find a special place in life and enjoy some recognition, and this desire to be "somebody" can haunt us because most of us intensely dislike obscurity.

Everyday we look for opportunities to be number one. One example is when we become radical sports fans and follow the number one team so we can feel the heady euphoria of being at the top.

But we can't trust appearances. Things are not always as they seem.

One summer Ron and I were traveling on a highway north of Phoenix on the way to the Grand Canyon. I was enjoying the scenery as Ron drove when suddenly a speeding, black Mercedes with a Nevada license plate whizzed past.

The car didn't make much of an impression on me at first as it passed, but then I did a double take. "Follow that car," I cried to Ron. "There's a dead woman lying in that back window."

Ron stepped on the gas until we were right behind the car. Sure enough, there was a woman dressed in shorts and T-shirt lying in the back window. Now as my detective instincts kicked in I asked, "Who killed that woman? Why is she in the back window?"

I enjoyed this mystery immensely.

Then Ron's logic took over. "If she is alive, she wouldn't be lying in the back window. If she is dead, she wouldn't be in the window either. They would stuff her in the trunk out of sight. So it must be a mannequin."

A mannequin. There was nothing exciting about that. I'm a famous sleuth, and I have a mystery to solve here. "If that's a mannequin, why didn't they just put it in the back seat?"

As the car sped out of sight, I had to let it rest. I still thought about it, though.

Yet, things are not always as they seem.

Things in life are not always as they seem, either. A person can be number one on the outside—rich, famous, and successful—but a failure on the inside, in the personal and spiritual parts of life.

Success is elusive

Most people don't realize that when "you get there," there's nothing there. However, you don't know that until you arrive.

We can think becoming number one, wealthy, and happy are all synonymous. They don't necessarily go together.

Yet, we work hard to surround ourselves with emblems that show we're number one and successful: large houses, expensive cars, designer clothes, and costly "toys." We try to create this image of success by acting and spending money like the "successful." And continue to order our lives according to the opinions and expectations of others of this philosophy.

When I was a teenager, I thought life was going to be a garden of roses: If I reached a certain level of success, I would live happily ever after.

Many adults live with this success stereotype and often spend a lifetime living others' expectations so they can become that star—to belong. So they're not left out.

However, you miss out when you're afraid of being left out.

Let's face it: True success and happiness are in the spiritual realm. If we can grasp this reality, we'll feel like number one. We'll feel successful. We won't spend wasted years pursuing the false. God wants us to have success in family, home, and work.

Success is not always associated with our interpretation of success.

One of the reasons we strive with this prosperity thinking is because we intensely dislike being labeled average or mediocre. If someone calls us mediocre, it's as if they called us a bad name. It's humiliating. However, mediocrity is relevant. What one person may consider average is for another person the best.

To seek for success or to avoid mediocrity rather than pursuing fulfillment produces the negative results of greed, pride, selfishness, and many other negatives. The world is full of people trying to accomplish something big, not realizing that life is made up of everyday little things.

Don't waste energy judging your own accomplishments. There will always someone better looking, smarter, more talented, and wealthier than you. These summits are forever beyond range.

The greatest success is not what you have done, but what God has done through you. Discover what God has given you—talents and intelligence—and use them to the best of your ability.

Few of us during a lifetime ever come near to exhausting the resources we have within.

Allow yourself to be at peace with yourself. God will enhance your talents and abilities so that you can accomplish anything He asks you to do.

Cease struggling and live.

Be fulfilled in who you are. Self-fulfillment is getting the most mileage and satisfaction out of your abilities. This is where your greatness lies. Concentrate your will and energies to the tasks given to you in your life.

Be what God made you to be. Nothing more. Nothing less. You don't have to be "the best." There's a freedom in letting ambition go and with it go the anger, anxiety, and disillusionment that accompany it.

You do not have to be other than what God created you—human. You are only obligated to do that for which God created you. Once you accept your limitations, you can begin to learn what God has in mind for you.

You'll soon discover what winning is.

Winning is

Often we have difficulty defining what winning is, because there are many "winners" who don't appear on the outside to be winning.

In 1907 Halbert Donovan, a wealthy financier from New York, came to see Edith Kohn on the prairies of South Dakota. She ran a store and a newspaper. Halbert came to finance pioneer ventures, but he came at a time when the settlers or homesteaders had just been through a severe drought. They had also fought against other unbelievable odds of dust storms, prairie fires, blizzards, and just making ends meet.

This is what he saw: parched earth, ruined crops, settlers' homes that looked like miserable huts in ghettos of cities, clutter of farm machinery and other junk left outdoors, countless barrels for hauling water, the inevitable pile of tin cans, and dreariness that was unbelievably ugly.

The outward had all the appearances of grim failure. However, when Halbert Donovan learned of the bravery and courage of these people, he knew in his heart they were winners.

The outward isn't the barometer that gauges winning or losing. It's what happens on the inside. What is invisible is what counts ultimately.

Winning is about winning.

15

How-to: Taking Action

God wants us to win, to be healthy and whole. To become spiritually fit. To adapt a winning lifestyle. God is on our side. We can't lose, because He can't lose.

One of the hardest things to do is to take action and become what you've learned and know how to be. God intends you to practice what you've absorbed from the Bible and to become what He intends for you. It won't happen without your choosing it. It takes a decision, an act of the will.

Just as life is sustained and growth is accomplished by good health habits, food and exercise; the Bible is the food and exercise for spiritual success through practical application of the Word.

There are some who desire new "thrills" to keep their spiritual experiences alive and base their lives on feelings and experiences. On the other hand, some are motivated by their thoughts and actions. Both groups of people think they are right.

It's like the age-old controversy: Which came first the chicken or the egg? Within the spiritual world a similar controversy endures: Which is most important, action or feelings?

Maybe it's something like desiring to take a trip. I can sit in my car all day in the garage and wait for feelings to take me to anywhere USA. The car will never deliver me until I choose action. I must open the garage door, get into the car, fit the key into the ignition, put it into gear, place my hands on the steering wheel, and press my foot on the gas. Presto. The vehicle is suddenly in motion. It will take me anywhere I desire.

It's action that comes first in a winning life. When I take action, then my feelings come around. I take action—whether I feel like it or not—and go into my "sanctuary," sit down in my chair, take time to love the Lord, pick up my Bible and converse with the Lord, ask of Him, listen to Him, and write down instructions I may receive from God. Then if God speaks to my heart about writing an email to a sorrowing parent or visiting a lonely neighbor, I'll do it whether I feel like it or not. Action is my best partner.

Winning is having God-given goals and a take-action plan to accomplish that purpose.

God-given goals

Some years ago my grandson Jonathan anticipated the great event, a new baby sister. She arrived with much joy and happiness for the family. Jonathan was disappointed in his sister Christie and told me one day, "Grandma, she can't even talk to me or play with me." Then he said with resolve as he stuck out his chin and put his shoulders back, "I'm going to teach her to talk."

He figured that if Christie could talk; they could play together. So he began by making his sister pronounce words. When she didn't say them properly, he'd tell her repeat them. Jonathan took every opportunity to drill her with words, then later he taught her phrases and sentences. Jonathan stayed true to his original purpose, and Christie learned to speak correctly in sentences before she was two. Soon Jonathan and Christie played together for hours. He discovered she was an intelligent companion. Now that they are adults, Jonathan may wish he hadn't been so diligent with his goals. Most of the time they get on very well.

Jonathan believed he could reach his goal. Believing is more important than the goal itself. All of us need a simple goal or goals. We need something to work toward.

There are two kinds of goals: peripheral goals and instinctive goals.

Peripheral goals

These are goals that are formed by outside influences. They are from without and are shaped by environment, family, and friends. They are fashioned by what others think someone should become rather than by what an individual knows intuitively.

Sometimes a well-meaning parent will inflict upon a child a peripheral goal, because it is a goal he or she, the parent, has always desired.

For instance, a father may inflict the goal of a son becoming a pro football player. The result of this son achieving this peripheral goal is not going to be positive, because persons with peripheral goals become artificial, restless, dissatisfied, and burn out easily. They often intensely dislike their work and their life.

Instinctive goals

These are goals that are formed from desires of the heart. They are from within. They are born in the soul. They fit perfectly with gifts, talents, temperament, and calling in life. They are the culmination of desires individuals are born and made for. Persons with instinctive goals are unique, content, and individualistic. They enjoy life and love what they do.

Three simple steps for goal setting

Start with communication with God. God will help you sort through and organize your thoughts and help you focus on the right, instinctive goals for your personal life. To have a goal means to have aim, design, or purpose. God will help you define goals that compliment God's purpose for your life.

Keep goals simple. The ideal is to target only one or two attainable goals and keep them realistic. Compare yourself only to yourself and be honest in your estimation of who you are and your energy level. Allow yourself to dream. Follow the dictates of your intuition and heart.

Write down your goals. Record these on paper and keep them in a safe place. Every few months look at this paper to remind yourself of your goals. If you set a goal, and see by the paper that you didn't attain it and never will, tear up the paper and start over. Just because goals are made and written down, doesn't mean they are irrevocable and cannot be changed. Change any goal at any time if a goal no longer fits you or your life.

Plan for Taking Action

After you have taken time to love the Lord—choosing, loving, conversing, asking—now is the opportunity for you to use and apply what you grasped with an action plan.

During a tour of Wind Cave in South Dakota, the lights are turned off for a time to demonstrate total darkness. It is frightening, because there is no color, no sense of direction, and no sight. Then the lights are turned back on. Blessed relief. There is color, direction, and sight again. When we communicate with God, He gives us illumination for taking action in our lives. He gives us color, direction, and sight.

Here is an optional, five-day guide for taking action in your life.

Day One: Take action in your personal life

Think of one way to be in God's realm today by applying the truth of the Scripture verse or verses you read and thought about when you conversed with God.

Options for new action

Let the heart of God touch you through the Scripture. Find pleasure in the things that please Him, joy in the things that delight Him, and contentment in the things that glorify Him.

Invite Him into your life every day. Jesus is not uncomfortable in the everyday, routine place of your life. He is relaxed in the midst of the ordinary. He doesn't need to be entertained; He enjoys being with you simply because you are

His. When you continually put the Word of God into your mind, the result of a modified, corrected, and strengthened person emerges. Use the Bible and the truths of the Bible in your daily life.

Allow your thoughts to dwell upon God often during a twenty-four hour period. Give thanks in all circumstances of life, as disheartening as they can be at times, and relax in God. He has a way of working everything out.

Day Two: Take action in your family life

Think of one way to apply your week's scripture verses in your family.

Options for new action

Create a positive atmosphere in your home. Try to practice principles from the verses you read every day in your home. Create a happy home with proper food and drink, rest, exercise, cleanliness, positive mental attitude, controlled and uplifting speech, good friends, daily prayer and Bible reading, a giving spirit, and the willingness of each family member to give of their time, love, talents, and gifts to the other family members.

Become accountable to someone. Life is complicated with so many values thrown at us. We need one another. We need each other's love and forgiveness. When the Bible tells us to love, let's love. When the Bible teaches us to forgive, let's forgive.

Day Three: Take action with your friends

Think of one way to apply your week's scripture verses in your relationship with friends.

Options for new action

Develop loving relationships. Take the initiative to do good things for your friends. Do a good deed without telling anyone, financially assist someone in need, deliver a prepared meal to a friend who is sick, and help with cleaning or maintenance for those who are unable.

Encourage others. Ask yourself, "What can I do to encourage someone today?" Does someone you know need comfort, a phone call, a kind word, or a smile? It's not the great things that are done in life, but the sum of little things that counts. Whenever a friend comes to mind, do something to bless them.

Day Four: Take action in your church

Think of one way to apply your week's scripture verses and take action in your church today. How can you serve in your church?

Options for new action in your church

Develop a servant attitude. We are all servants with a ministry. God does not have special people for ministry; God has special ministry for people. We serve God because He's God.

Serve God with submission. Come as a servant to get orders, not to give them. Come to Him as a child. Make sure your heart is pure before God.

Day Five: Take action in your world

Think of one way to apply your week's scripture verses in your world.

Options for new action in your world

Look for opportunities. God's best gifts to us are not things, but opportunities. When we begin to apply God's word to our service in the world, we'll see opportunities. Seeing the opportunities can make us uncomfortable, and we try to protect ourselves from discomfort and changes. But an inevitable part of life on earth is change. Constant change.

Trust the Lord for answers. In our world the values are constantly shifting. We are not to change the Word to fit our lifestyle; we are to change our lifestyle to fit the Word. We are to hear the Word, then put it into practice. Practice until your spiritual muscles perform. Read God's instructions about how to live. Then accept them, feel inspired by them, affirm them as truth, and live them in your world.

Give winning a chance. Not to see if it works, but to see how well it works.

Winning With God Minute Manager

(Allow a few minutes a day.)

Day One: Take action in your personal life.
Day Two: Take action in your family life.
Day Three: Take action with your friends.
Day Four: Take action in your church.
Day Five: Take action in your world.

16

Benefit: Self-actualization

Self-actualization is: Knowing who you are and what you are here for and overcoming every obstacle to achieve that intention. It is the highest need on the hierarchy scale for human beings. It is the benefit of winning. Choosing to communicate with God and letting God work in our minds and hearts enables us to become self-actualized.

In this win-win situation it's possible to develop into what God made us to be, what God designed us to be. Living within God's plan is not without its challenges, but it does leave us with a sense of peace and rightness in what we are doing. Peace and happiness come from living a simple, useful life.

God will never ask you to be someone or something you cannot be. Whatever assignment God gives you to do, just be yourself and let him use you.

Enhance your personality and achieve your full potential by allowing Christ to live through you by letting Him direct your thoughts, actions, and words. This is self-actualizing or peak performance.

The apostle John wrote about peak performance God desired for the seven churches of Asia in the Book of Revelation, chapters 2 and 3. The seven churches were actual churches in the cities mentioned: Ephesus, Smyrna, Pergamos, Thyratira, Sardis, Philadelphia, and Laodicea.

Bible scholars agree that these letters to the churches may be interpreted historically, pastorally, or practically. I choose to interpret them practically in the text of this book with ongoing application urging all of us to become peak performers through communication with God.

Winners or peak performers live in their potential and are able to demonstrate the following seven hidden secrets or mysteries of life that the churches in Revelation 2 and 3 possessed or needed: love, courage, determination, purity, alertness, perseverance, and enthusiasm.

Ephesus: The secret of love

Love is unconditional acceptance.
Love ceases judgment; just loves.

Options for performance

Love from the center of who you are. Present genuine love in everything you do and to everyone you meet. Love freely with no conditions.

Whatever you find to do, love it. Whatever your course in life, do it for the love of it. For without love, there is nothing.

Smyrna: The secret of courage

Courage is moving ahead when scared to death.
Courage holds steady in hard times.

Options for performance

Courage progresses in spite of obstacles. It accepts the challenge of life's calling with confidence. Setbacks may just be small corrections in your course, to give new understanding or as a test. Take courage. Attacks and disappointments are only minor setbacks. "This too shall pass."

Be ready. God will bring you to the kingdom for "such a time as this." Your courage to hold steady in the hard times will be an example to help others out of their misery. You will weep with those who weep. You will help them rise again until joy and laughter are restored to their lives.

Pergamos: The secret of determination

Determination is firmness of purpose.
Determination never compromises original identity.

Options for performance

God will reveal meaning and purpose to you. He will give you a reason for being on earth. Everyone needs meaning in life. When life has meaning, fulfillment and joy are experienced.

Be connected to God so you can stay true to your original identity. This will give you amazing insights into everyday happenings that will cause a positive process of change in you. With food stored up from the Scriptures, you will climb from status quo into worthwhile influence over many people.

Thyratira: The secret of purity

Purity is cleanness and transparency.

Purity is creative integrity.

Options for performance

Purity is a subconsciousness that comes from life's experience. You can be born to wealth, beauty, and intelligence, but you're not born into the peak performance of purity. It has to be attended to. It takes getting up after falling down. Someone said, "Man's greatest triumph is not in falling, but in rising each time he falls." This is what power of purity is able to do for you—lift you up when you are down.

Purity displays strength on the inside—integrity. Often this strength is evident in leadership and organization. This power of purity can create order out of chaos and make something out of nothing. You were created to create. When you are creative, you are representing the highest degree of emotional health and purity.

Sardis: The secret of alertness

Alertness watches for opportunities.

Alertness diligently guards what is treasured.

Options for performance

Grasp opportunity. Opportunity is contained within every problem of life. Every problem is the seed of an opportunity for some greater benefit. Act immediately. You can open up a whole new range of possibilities for your life.

Be alert to the small miracles of the simple things of life: home, food, comfortable bed, companionship, healthy children, and the beauty of God's creation. Pay attention to the little things. Celebrate life.

Philadelphia: The secret of perseverance

Perseverance is never giving up.
Perseverance walks through open doors.

Options for performance

Work diligently at whatever your hand finds to do. Finish every assignment you start. The most rewarding things in life are often the ones that look like they cannot be done. God will set in motion extraordinary situations in everyday surroundings to ease the completion of the job.

Embrace the open door of serving even when you're weary. Each door of life can be perceived as an exit or an entrance. Choose to see the open door as an entrance to positive changes.

Laodicea: The secret of enthusiasm

Enthusiasm is vitality and fervency.
Enthusiasm anticipates a fulfilling life.

Options for performance

Spontaneously administer random acts of kindness. This will kill boredom and restore vitality and fervency. You were born to give, as all creation is. Flowers give beauty. Birds give songs. Fruit trees give fruit. Enthusiastically believe in contributing to the care of others.

Let go of security in things, ideas, and positions. Security is connected to the past; it's about something you already know. Rather anticipate a great road to a fulfilling life. Whatever you do, leave a positive improvement upon your job or position. Leave your mark on the world around you. No one else can leave the same positive force as you can because of your uniqueness.

Self-actualization

Today God has you where He wants you. He has guided every detail of your life. There is no luck or karma that governs you. God gave you talents. They are God's gifts to you. How you use those talents is your gift to God. You will look back on your life and say, "It is good. I did what God wanted me to do." That's self-actualization.

Be willing to close some chapters and willingly go on to new ones. Be ready for new heights. New things await you. God delights in turning the pages of your life so that He can write exciting new chapters.

Communicate with God anywhere and at any time. Treasure your friendship with the God of the universe who desires to commune with you.

Communicate with God and you will overcome the obstacles of choosing God, loving God, conversing with God, asking of God and winning with God. All your basic needs—survival, security, love, self-esteem, and self-actualization—will be fulfilled.

Positive Affirmations

(Say these aloud or to yourself.)

God calls me not for what I am, but for what I am going to become when He completes me!

I am winning!
I am more than surviving!

Communication with God Weekly Schedule

Day 1

1. **Choose a time** _____ AM or PM.

2. **Focus on one characteristic of God**: 2-3 minutes.
Attributes of God: (choose one)
Self-existent: God has no origin. He is self dependent.
Self-sufficient: God is what He is in Himself, the I Am. Eternal: God is unending in existence.
Infinite: God is limitless, measureless.
Immutable: God never changes. He is not developing. Omniscient: God is all wise.
Omnipotent: God is all powerful.
Omnipresent: God is present everywhere.
Transcendent: There is none like God. He is exalted.
Faithful: God never fails.
Good: God bestows us with blessings everyday.
Just: Safety is guaranteed to all who put their trust in Him.
Mercy: Because of God's mercies we are not consumed.
Grace: God grants us undeserved favor.
Love: God is our friend. He first loved us.
Holy: God's holiness is complete order, nothing lacking. Sovereign: God is free to do whatever He wills.

3. **Read Bible and think** about verses: 5-10 minutes.

4. **Make specific requests for yourself**: 5 minutes.

5. **Take action in your personal life** by applying Scripture: all day.

Day 2

1. **Choose a time** _____ AM or PM.

2. **Focus on one name of Christ**: 2-3 minutes

Advocate, Alpha, Anointed One, Apostle, Author

Beginning, Beloved, Bread of life, Bridegroom

Captain, Chief Cornerstone, Christ, Counselor, Creator

Dayspring, Daystar, Defender, Deliverer, Door

Elect, Ensign, Eternal Life, Everlasting Father

Faithful Witness, Finisher of our Faith, Friend

Gift of God, Glorious Lord, Good Shepherd, Guide,

Head of the Church, Healer, High Priest, Holy One, Hope

I Am, Intercessor, Inheritance, Immanuel, Immortal

Jehovah-Jireh, Jesus, Judah, Judge, Just One

King, King Everlasting, King of Glory, King of Kings

Lamb of God, Life, Light, Lion of Judah, Lord of Glory

Master, Mercy Seat, Messenger, Messiah, Mighty God

Name above Every Name, Never-failing Guide, Nazarene

Offering, Omega, Overcomer

Physician, Priest, Prophet, Prince of Peace

Quest of my Soul, Quiet Place

Redeemer, Refiner, Refuge, Resurrection, Righteousness

Savior, Shepherd, Son of God, Son of Man

Teacher, Temple, Treasure, Tree of Life, Truth

Very Present Help in Time of Trouble, Vine

Way, Witness, Word, Wonderful Counselor, Worthy

3. **Read Bible and look up words** in a dictionary: 5-10 minutes.

4. **Make specific requests for your family**: 5-8 minutes.

5. **Take action by applying Scripture to family life**: all day.

Day 3

1. **Choose a time** _____ AM or PM.

2. **Focus on the Holy Spirit** (Come, Holy Spirit): 1 minute.

3. **Read Bible and ask questions**: 5-10 minutes.

4. **Make specific requests for your friends**: 5 minutes.

5. **Take action with your friends** by applying Scripture: all day.

Day 4

1. **Choose a time** _____ AM or PM.

2. **Read a favorite psalm** or portion of a psalm aloud: 2-3 minutes.

3. **Read the Bible and just listen** to what God says: 5-10 minutes.

4. **Make specific requests for your church**: 5 minutes.

5. **Take action in your church** by applying Scripture: all day.

Day 5

1. **Choose a time** _____ AM or PM

2. **Express your love** to the Lord: 1 minute.

3. **Read Bible and summarize** or do any of the above: 5-10 minutes.

4. **Make specific requests for your world**: 5 minutes.

5. **Take action in your world** by applying Scripture: all day.

Day 6

Meditate upon Scripture during free thought times, and ask of God when individual requests come to mind.

Day 7

Meditate upon Scripture during free thought times, and ask of God when individual requests come to mind.

Acknowledgments

Many thanks to:

The men and women who attended "More than Survival" seminars and classes and provided me with responses and reinforcement.

My family: daughter Karen Westerfield, son-in-law Tim Westerfield, daughter JoAnn Ellis, and son-in-law Reid Ellis for advice, editing, and ever-present support.

My husband Ron for his love and suggestions through all my projects.

Other books by LaVonne Masters

The Bible Verse Book

Memorize and Meditate

Successful Living:
Memorizing and Meditating

Some through the Flood
(Coauthored by Ron and LaVonne Masters)